THIS REAL ESTATE AGENT WILL WORK FOR TACOS

This journal belongs to:

_____

Copyright ©2019 **Real Estate Bizzy Trends** All Rights Reserved. Reproduction and distribution of the contents, statements or images in this book without written permission by the author is prohibited.